KTNG
WBBL
KLNG
WHERE'D GRANDPA GO?
THIS IS ALL THAT HE LEFT...

DEADMAN WONDERLAND

STORY & ART BY JINSEI KATAOKA, KAZUMA KONDOU

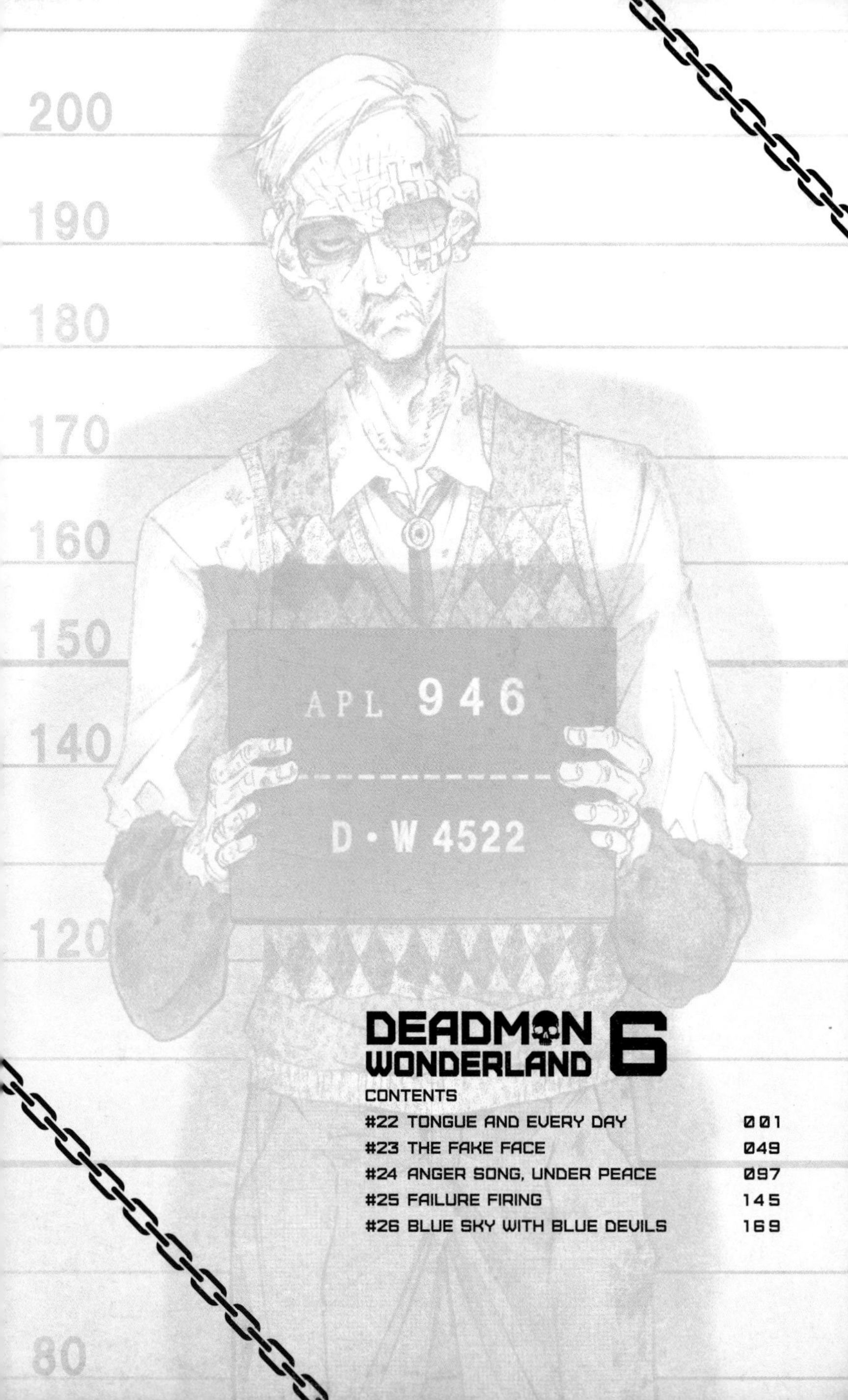

DEADMAN WONDERLAND 6

CONTENTS

WHAT A WEIRD KID!
HE WAS ROLLING AROUND SAYING HIS CHEST HURT.
YEAH, I SAW.
AND HE HAD A WEIRD MARK ON HIS CHEST.
CREEPY!
I'VE NEVER SEEN A DEADMAN LIKE HIM BEFORE.
12
TIK
WAKE-UP TIME!

COME OUTTA THERE, KID!
YOUR WEEK OF SOLITARY CONFINEMENT'S OVER.
CREEEK
...
ONE WEEK ...?
IT WAS LONG SO YOU WOULDN'T GIVE UP ANY DETAILS ABOUT THE ESCAPEES.

I HAD NO IDEA...
...IT'D BEEN SO LONG SINCE NAGI'S DEATH.
DEADMAN WONDERLAND
DEADMANWONDERLAND
HUH?
HMM
MRMR
OOOH
EARTH

DEADMAN WONDERLAND
PRIVATE PRISON
OR LAWLESS FREAK SHOW?
Hard as it may be to believe, these images...
...are not from a movie or violent computer game.
YOUTUBE
TOD
What you are seeing is real, film taken at an underground laboratory...
...where it's said these people are infected with a unique disease.
10:22
PRIVATE P
OR LAWLESS FRE

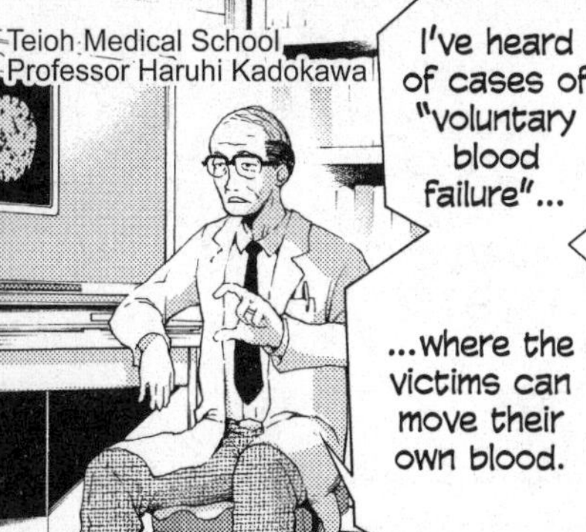

Teioh Medical School Professor Haruhi Kadokawa
I've heard of cases of "voluntary blood failure"...
...where the victims can move their own blood.

WHOA
It's only been seen in Japan.
And the patients have all gone missing. So the cause and course of the infection are still unknown.
WHUH

What do you mean by "missing"?
Data Chip sent to Media
Deadman Wonderland's Underground Lab
4 Name: Username Private: 2024/06/13 (Thur.) 10:32:57 ID: BVpb40d6—Mr. Kidnapper and
Burglar have finally done it. Template>>Past 2
295 Name: Username Private: 2024/06/13 (Thur.) 11:59:41 ID: DAah3evB—If this is for real it's
the biggest tragedy since the Great Tokyo Earthquake. It's way beyond a scandal!
296 Name: Username Private: 2024/06/13 (Thur.) 11:00:15 ID: tOBeTh—
296 Name: Username Private: 2024/06/13 (Thur.) 11:00:49 ID: 5rwJ6
They all just stopped going to their treatment sessions and stopped answering any outside contacts.

CLICK
Any chance they are all secretly being kept underneath Deadman Wonderland?

HEY! GET BACK IN LINE!
WUMP
THE MEDICAL EXAMS HAVE ALREADY STARTED!

...
THEY SAID SOME GUY USED HIS BLOOD TO BREAK DOWN A WALL. I GUESS IT'S TRUE.
HMMM
THERE ARE RUMORS OF AN UNDER-GROUND LAB.
HUH!
...
12th Periodic Medical Examination

...
THAT STORY... IS IT TRUE?
DID THE PROMOTER END THE INVESTIGATIONS OF ALL THOSE ACCIDENTS?
DON'T BE AN IDIOT.
SHUT DOWN THE NETWORK AND ALL THE MONITORS IN THE CELLS.
Y-YES, MA'AM ...
...

...TO GET CONTROL BACK FROM THAT FOX!

HMM———…

...
WHAT'S WRONG, GANTA...?
MMPH
YOU HAVEN'T BEEN EATING.
I'M FINE...
YOU SAW THE NEWS, DIDN'T YOU? KARAKO DID THAT.
SO NOW IT'S MY TURN TO DO WHAT'S RIGHT, ISN'T IT?
...
SMUSH

TH- THAT WAS THE LAST ONE!
CHNK
AND IT'S SO GOOD!
HUH?
OH. SORRY.
I COULDN'T TELL IT WAS A SNACK.

I...
I COULDN'T TASTE ANYTHING.

THAT'S HOW HE'S BEEN...

GANTA'S ACTING WEIRD!
WHAT DO I DO?
WAAAA
...
OH... YOU'RE SHIRO...
...THAT STUPID VIRGIN'S... I MEAN GANTA'S FRIEND.

DON'T GET TOO CLOSE! SHE'S A MONSTER!
HUH? WHAT'S HE PISSING HIS PANTS ABOUT?
You know her, don't you?

SO WHAT YOU'RE SAYING IS...
...YOU WANT TO CHEER GANTA UP, BUT YOU DON'T KNOW WHY HE'S UNHAPPY.
YEAH...
THEN, HOW ABOUT ...
...TELLING HIM EVERY DAY THAT HE'S "A DIRTY LITTLE COCKROACH THAT'S NOT EVEN WORTH DISPLAYING AT A PARASITE MUSEUM" OR...
..."IF YOU WERE A WEAPON, YOU'D BE ABOUT AS GOOD AS A WOODEN STICK."
IF I WERE YOU, I'D SPARE NO EFFORT TO TURN THAT ANNOYING, INNOCENT WIMP INTO A BROKEN LOST SOUL.
That sounds kinda complicated...
IF I KNEW WHAT THE CAUSE WAS, I COULD CREATE AN EVEN MORE EFFECTIVE TRAUMA.
MiNATSUKi...
I DON'T GET IT...

WE FINALLY MADE UP...

...BUT WHEN HE'S NOT HAPPY, IT FEELS TIGHT RIGHT HERE.

MAYBE SOMETHING'S WRONG WITH ME, TOO.

HI! ♥
WHOA
WHO SAID YOU COULD COME IN HERE?
A WOMAN CRIES PEARLS... A MAN SWEATS DIAMONDS...
THE ONE WHO KNOWS...
...WHAT IT'S LIKE TO WEAR BOTH JEWELS IS ME! CHOPLIN SUKEGAWA!
HELPING GIRLS IN LOVE—THAT'S MY LIFE'S WORK!
LEAVE IT TO US!
US...?

WOW! IT'S SO PRETTY!
WHAT IS THIS?
WHAT IS THIS?!
A FOOD-PREP UNIFORM, NATURALLY.
IT'S SHIRO, ISN'T IT?
LOOK.
BLOOP
CHAK
WSK
WSK
THE REASON HE CAN'T TASTE ANYTHING...
...IS THAT SOMETHING'S MISSING.

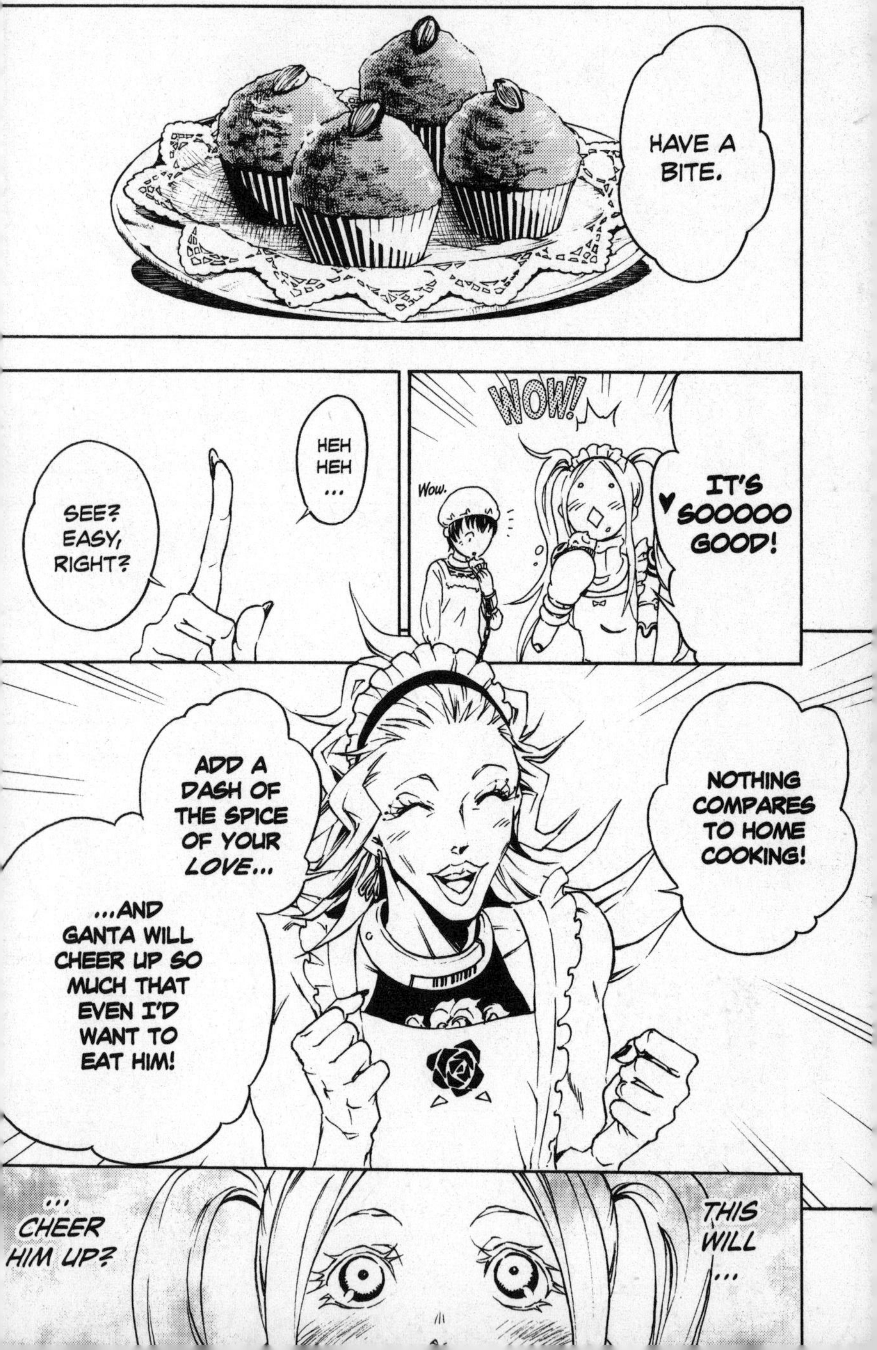

WOW!

IT'S SOOOOO GOOD!

Wow.

HEH HEH ...

SEE? EASY, RIGHT?

NOTHING COMPARES TO HOME COOKING!

ADD A DASH OF THE SPICE OF YOUR *LOVE*...

...AND GANTA WILL CHEER UP SO MUCH THAT EVEN I'D WANT TO EAT HIM!

THIS WILL ...

... CHEER HIM UP?

SO LET'S START COOKING!!
YESSIR!
Cookies?
TH
U
UMM... DID I MESS UP A LITTLE?
NOT JUST A LITTLE.
WAIT! LET ME FIND A TEST SUBJECT.

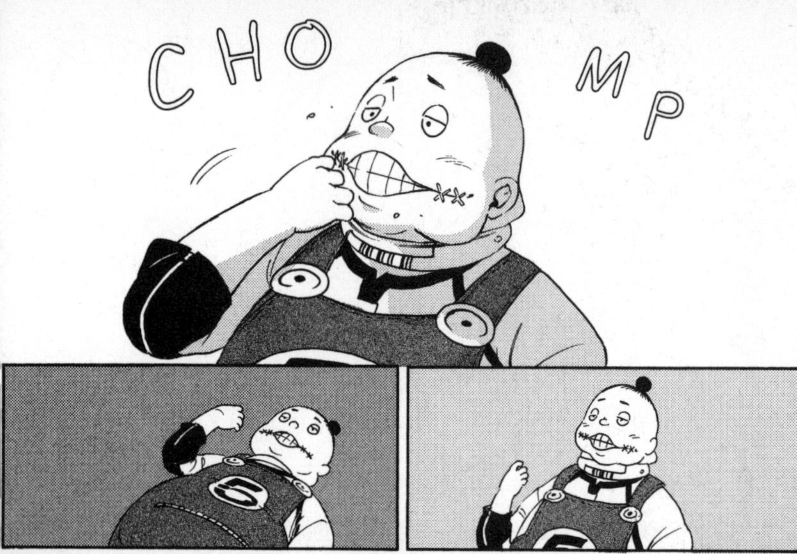
CHOMP

FROTH
URK
ACK
Y-YOU KNOCKED MASU OUT!
WHO KNEW THAT WAS EVEN POSSIBLE?
GRG

ALL RIGHT. MAYBE COOKING ISN'T YOUR THING, SHIRO.
WHAT ...?

THEN HOW...
...CAN I CHEER GANTA UP?
HONEY... I'M NOT...

I'LL DO ANYTHING!
ANYTHING!
...
KOFF
URGH
KOFF
WHAT'S WRONG, SENJI?

HUH?
YOU DON'T SMELL THAT?
...?

...
HAVE YOU LOST WEIGHT, GANTA?
YOU DON'T LOOK RIGHT.

...?
I HAVEN'T BEEN EATING MUCH.
THE RATIONS TASTE BAD.
ACTUALLY, THEY DON'T HAVE ANY TASTE.

OH, BUT I'M DOING OKAY.
...
WHAT'S THAT, THEN... A FASHION STATEMENT?

HUH ...?

... YOU...

YOU WERE FRIENDS WITH OWL, RIGHT?

THAT'S WHY...

...I *HAVE TO* GET OVER IT.

HMM ...

WANNA START TRAINING AGAIN?

AN ANT COULD KICK YOUR ASS RIGHT NOW.

IT'S JUST THAT...

... I'M ...

... SCARED.

BUT I'VE...
...JUST GONE ON LIVING LIKE NORMAL. EVERYONE ELSE HAS TOO.
LIKE NOTHING HAPPENED.
WE WERE TRYING TO...
...CHANGE THE WORLD, BUT IT'S LIKE NOTHING HAPPENED.
I'M SCARED OF THE WAY THE DAYS NEVER CHANGE.
I...

...
DID YOU FORGET WHERE YOU ARE?!

YOU SAW THE NEWS.

OWL CAUSED THAT CHANGE.

ONLY A STUPID KID WOULD THINK NOTHING'S CHANGED.

YOU JUST CAN'T SEE WHERE YOU STAND OR WHAT'S HAPPENING AROUND YOU.

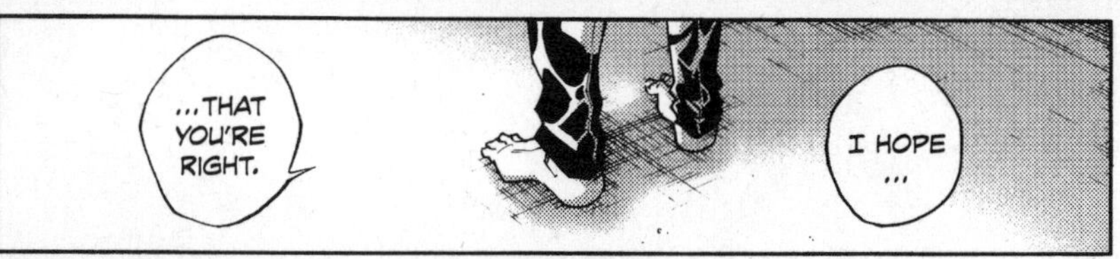

I HOPE ...
...THAT YOU'RE RIGHT.

Periodic Medical Examination
Nos. 3500 –

...

NEXT PATIENT.

Compatible Persons List

NUMBER 3733, AZAMI MIDO.

OKAY, TAKE A DEEP BREATH.

UM...
ARE YOU GOING TO GIVE ME AN INJECTION?
I DON'T THINK I GOT ONE DURING THE LAST EXAM.
REALLY ...?
NOTHING TO WORRY ABOUT. IT'S JUST ...
...A BOOSTER SHOT.
...

WHAT DID I DO TO GET CALLED IN?
THE ONLY THING WRONG WITH YOU IS YOUR ATTITUDE.
I CAN'T TELL YOU EVERY-THING...
...BUT THIS FACILITY HAS A SECRET UNDERGROUND SECTION CALLED *G WARD.*
WHAT?
UNDER-GROUND...?
IS THAT WHAT THOSE TWO WERE LOOKING FOR...?
ALL INMATES WHO POSSESS A CERTAIN *ABILITY* ARE HOUSED THERE.
THERE WEREN'T ENOUGH OF THEM TO SATISFY TAMAKI, AND WE BELIEVE HE'S CONDUCTING EXPERIMENTS TO CREATE OTHERS WITH THAT ABILITY.

YOU ARE ON THE LIST OF POTENTIAL EXPERIMENTAL CANDIDATES.
WHAT?!
WHY...?!
PTK
WEAR THIS.
YOUR COLLAR'S GPS DOESN'T WORK UNDER-GROUND.
THIS WILL TELL US EXACTLY WHERE YOU ARE.
G WARD...
...THE PATH TO THE FOX'S DEN.

NO NEED TO BE AFRAID.

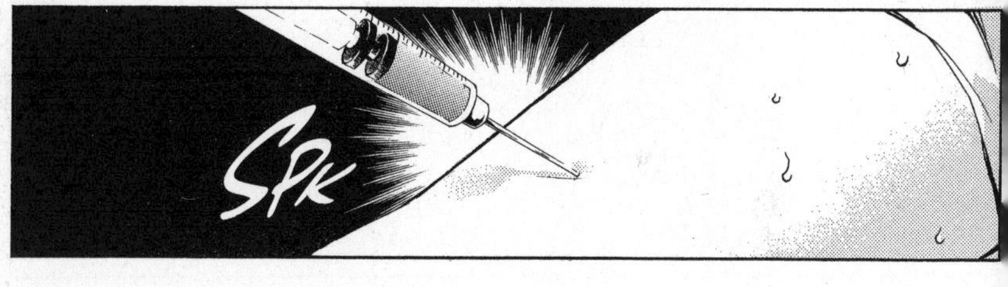

IT STILL HURTS.

IS THAT AN AFTER-EFFECT OF...?

KTANG
BANG
KLANG
CRASH
HMM ...?
WHY CAN'T I DO THIS?
SHIRO ...?
What's she wearing?
WHAT'RE THEY DOING HERE SO LATE AT NIGHT?
IS THAT SUPPOSED TO BE... FOOD?
WELL... SHE DID SAY SHE WAS OUT OF SNACKS.

YOU CAN TRY ALL YOU WANT, BUT NOTHING'S GONNA CHANGE.

NO MATTER WHAT YOU DO, IT'S LIKE IT NEVER HAPPENED.

CHAKKA

KTANG

WHEW.

I HOPE *THIS* WILL CHEER GANTA UP!

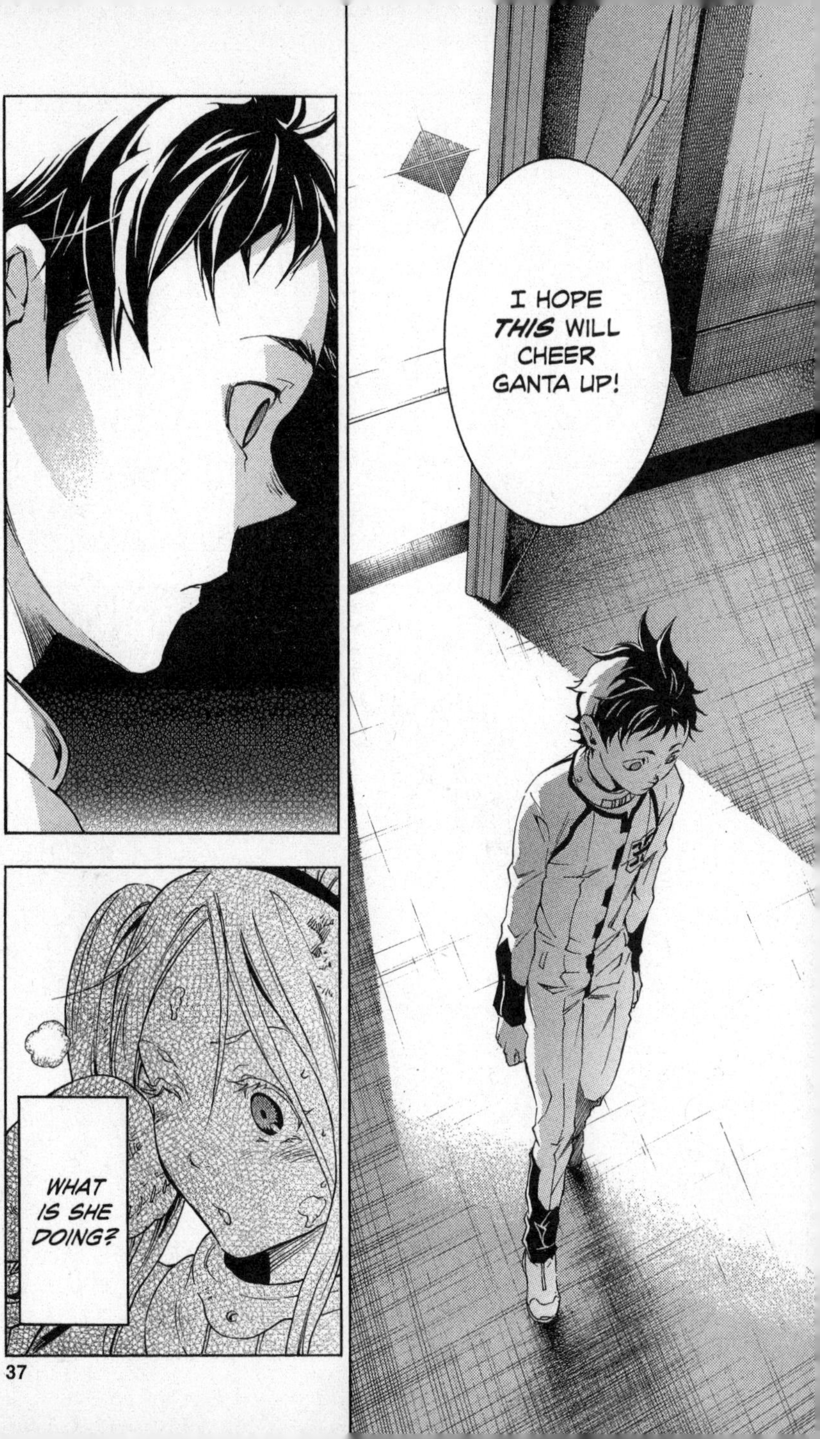

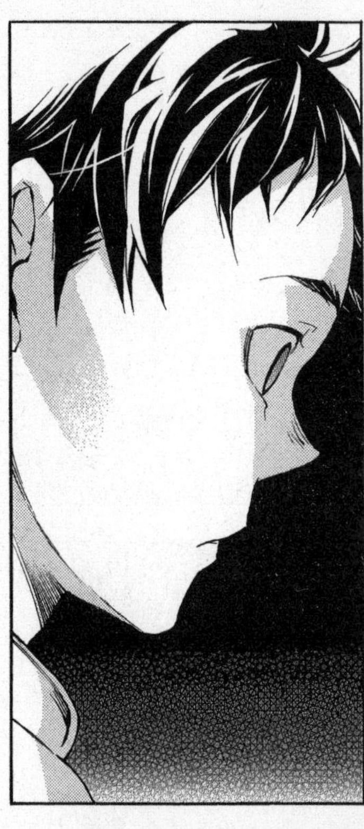

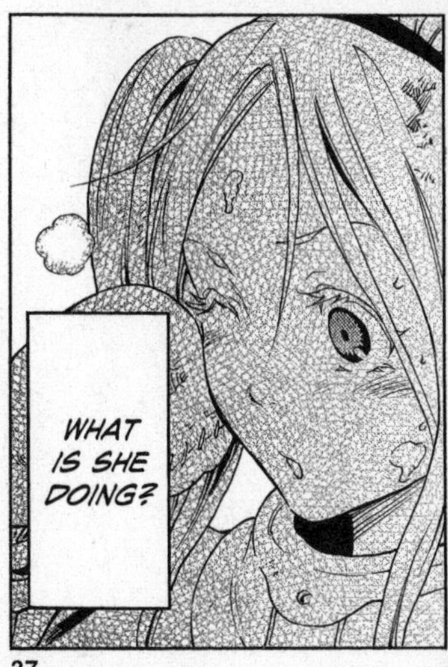
WHAT IS SHE DOING?

SHE'S USUALLY IN BED BY NOW.
HER LEG'S NOT FULLY HEALED, EITHER.
YOU JUST CAN'T SEE WHERE YOU STAND OR WHAT'S HAPPENING AROUND YOU.
...
WHAT-EVER...

MMMF...
G1-02

YAWN...
OH... GOOD MORNING, GANTA.
SHE LOOKS AWFUL!
OH, THAT'S... UM...
TODAY'S RATIONS. THEY CAME EARLY...
AND THEY SAID...
...THEY'RE A LITTLE MESSY.
...
GANTA ...
ARE YOU NOT GOING TO EAT AGAIN TODAY?

...

I'LL EAT.

T K

OH, AND THEY SAID...

...THEY MIGHT TASTE MESSY TOO!

HOLD ON...

B-DMP

B-DMP

B-DMP

THIS IS GOOD!

REALLY?!
TAK
YEAH.
A BIT SWEET, BUT TASTY.
I THOUGHT I'D NEVER TASTE ANYTHING AGAIN.
NOM
HOW ...?
WHEW
OH, GOOD.
GGURRGRLG
KLKE
HUH?
OH, RIGHT ...
I DIDN'T GET TO EAT YESTERDAY.

OH...

THEN LET'S EAT THIS TOGETHER!

HEH HEH ...

OKAY!

TODAY IS DIFFERENT THAN YESTERDAY...

BUT LIFE CHANGES BIT BY BIT EVERY DAY.

SECONDS!
BURP
SHNNG
Hmm?
SHIRO... WHERE'S MY SHARE?

SKRCH SKRCH

WHAT'S WRONG?

MY ARM ITCHES WHERE I GOT THAT SHOT.

SHOT?

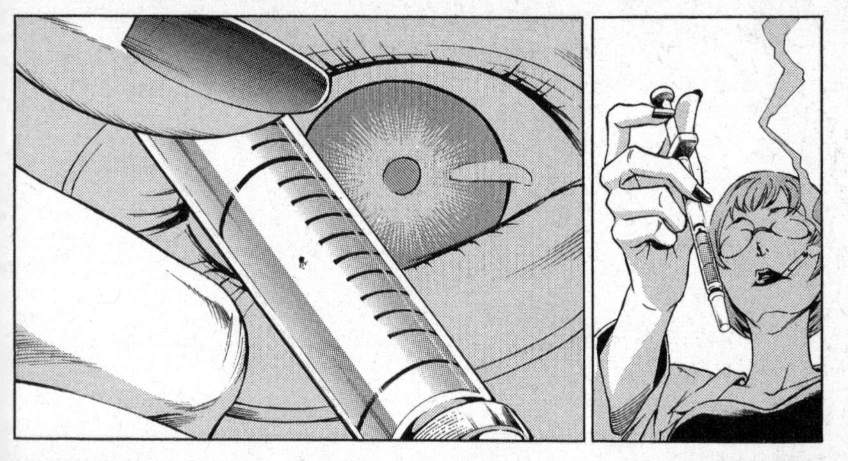

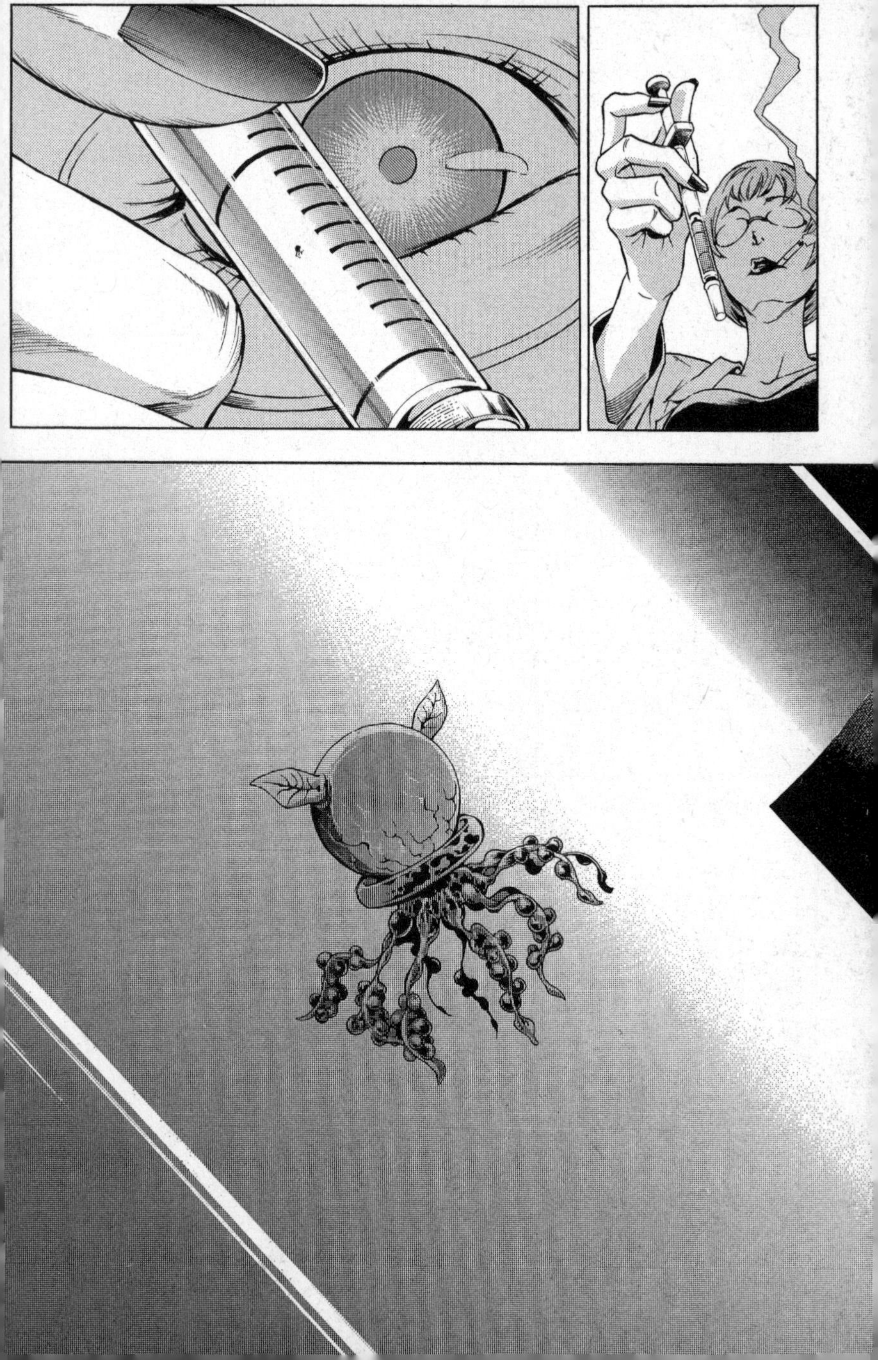

DEAD
MAN
WONDER LAND

23 The Fake Face
DEADMAN WONDERLAND
DEADMAN WONDERLAND
B33
B13
B15
UGH...
URGH...
SHVR
SHK
SHVR
ZWRRR
GUARD ...
I DON'T FEEL SO GOOD...

23 The Fake Face

MINISTRY OF DEFENS

IT'S ALREADY BEEN A MONTH SINCE...

...THE EXISTENCE OF THE DEADMEN WAS LEAKED TO THE PRESS.

THERE'S ONLY SO MUCH I CAN DO TO KEEP MY SUPERIORS QUIET.
I ALREADY APOLOGIZED PROFUSELY FOR THAT.
I'M NOT GETTING ON MY KNEES AGAIN.
NEXT TIME TRY DISEM-BOWELING YOURSELF.
GOOD. YOU'RE DEVELOPING A SENSE OF HUMOR, MAJOR AOHI.

WHY? IS SOMETHING FUNNY?
...
SWP
SWP
YOU'LL FIND OUT AT TOMORROW'S PRESS CONFERENCE.
TEK

AT THE FIRST APPEARANCE OF THE NINBEN ...

DEADMEN?

I HEAR THEY'RE KILLING EACH OTHER EVERY NIGHT.

WISH THEY'D JUST EXECUTE 'EM ALREADY.

IDIOT! WHAT IF THEY HEAR YOU!

IT'S SOME KIND OF DISEASE, ISN'T IT?

IT'S SO SCARY.

A MURDER DISEASE?

HOW AWFUL!

Deadman Wo
CIRCUS
HMMM...
I'M KINDA FEVERISH...
KYOO?
BMP
BMP
KINCHO!
NO.
YOU GET FED AFTER PRACTICE!
KYOO
KYOO!
HMPH!

WHSSH

ALL RIGHT.
TOOT
READY...
SET...
KRAK
TK TK

GO!
PONK

CLAP CLAP
CLAP CLAP
CLAP
!
CLAP

YOU'RE ...

THE DEADMEN ARE ABOVE-GROUND?!

YES ...
I SAW A NUMBER OF FACES FROM THE FILES...
This one next!
On my CP!

G WARD... HAS BEEN OPENED?!

MRRM
HMMM
HEY... WHAT IS THIS...?
NOW OF ALL TIMES?
IT'S NOT A TRAP, IS IT?

CAN WE JUST GO...?
MMM...

I HAVEN'T DONE ANY SUNBATHING IN A LONG TIME.

BUT I GUESS YOU WOULDN'T KNOW WHAT THAT'S LIKE.

OF COURSE I DO.

MY DAUGHTER'S VOICE KNOWS ALL.

TAP

BUT SHE DOESN'T SEEM TO KNOW WHAT THE PROMOTER'S UP TO...

'COURSE NOT. SHE'S NOT GOD.

ANYWAY, I'M KINDA DIGGIN' A WIND THAT DOESN'T SMELL LIKE BLOOD.

STAFF ONLY

WHAT IS TAMAKI THINKING?

OH YEAH.
JUST HAD CHOCOLATE-COVERED RICE.
?!
...
THAT'S HARD-CORE!
You got balls.
HEH HEH ...
...
YOU SEEM ...
... DIFFERENT.
REALLY?
...
A LOT'S HAPPENED ...

YOU...
...JUST KINDA DISAPPEARED ALL OF A SUDDEN.
IS IT TRUE YOU WENT "UNDERGROUND"?
WHAT?
HEY, YOU DON'T HAVE THAT...
...THAT *THING* EVERYBODY'S BEEN TALKING ABOUT?
!
BOOP
KYOO!
KYOO!
PUNT

KYOO!
BOOT
HA HA HA!
PASS! PASS!
PUNT
HA HA HA! THIS GUY'S TOUGH.
LET'S PLAY BASEBALL INSTEAD!
...
WHAT THE HELL DO YOU THINK YOU'RE DOING?!
OH, I'M SO SCARED.
SNORK
KOO
YOU CAN HAVE HIM BACK. JUST...
SWIP
...CATCH!
!

BAM
YOINK
KYOO...
WOBBLE
KYOOO?!
WBBL
SORRY, MY HAND SLIPPED.
AH HA HA! AWESOME!
KINCHO!

Kyooo
HOW AM I GONNA GET HIM DOWN...?
HANG ON, KINCHO!
...
SCHH
STAND BACK.

ZWCH

...!!

ZWSSSH

KRAK
KYOO?
KTNG
KYOO!
WUMP
KLANG
KRASH
PNNG
OWW ...

I'M STILL FEELING THE EFFECTS...
OHH
WHA...?!
H-HIS BLOOD M-MOVED!!
N-NO WAY!
THAT KID, IS HE...
...ONE OF THOSE "DEAD-GUYS"?!
H-HE...
HE'S A *MONSTER!*
AAAAH!

...THEY'LL THINK...

...THAT YOU'RE A DEADMAN LIKE ME.

WHAT'S YOUR NAME ...?
ME ...?
I'M GANTA IGARASHI.
GANTA, HUH?
GO WITH THAT.
CALLING YOURSELF "DEADMAN" IS KINDA LAME.
TH-THANKS, MS. AZAMI ...

FLOP
TMP
JUST AZAMI IS FINE.
I'M NOT SO FORMAL.

HERE.
YOU SAID "OUCH."
PUT THIS BAND-AID ON IT.

I DUNNO... IT'S KINDA GIRLY.
Not really my style...
...
IT'S JUST A STUPID SHAPE! WHAT DOES IT MATTER?!

THANKS.
BUT I'M FINE.
MY PAIN'S ON THE INSIDE.

SWP
OH. MISS AZA-
I MEAN, AZAMI... YOU'RE HURT TOO.

TUG
!

HERE.
SPK

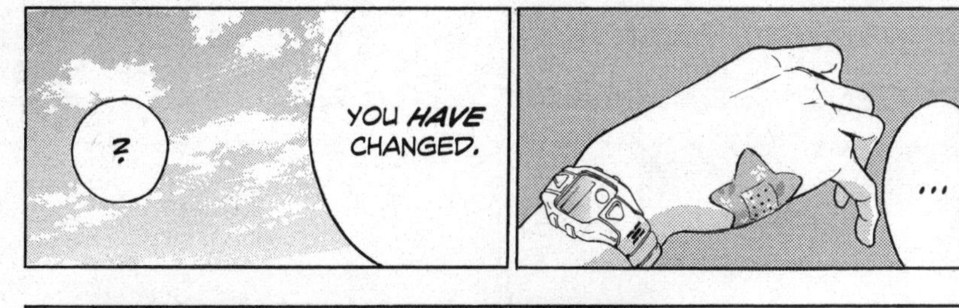
...
YOU *HAVE* CHANGED.
?

I'M SAYING YOU'VE BECOME A REAL SMOOTH OPERATOR!

SWFF
GASP!
OH...
DON'T LET IT GO TO YOUR HEAD! YOU AREN'T *THAT* SMOOTH!
ZWIP
I...
I HAVE TO FINISH RE-HEARSING!
G-GOTTA G-GO...
WO OOOM

I'M GONNA ...
...GO TO THE INFIRMARY.
SKFF
I'M SORRY, BUT...
...WOULD YOU...
KYOO?
...KEEP AN EYE ON KINCHO?

YEAH ...
SURE ...
KYOO...

ZZW
OT

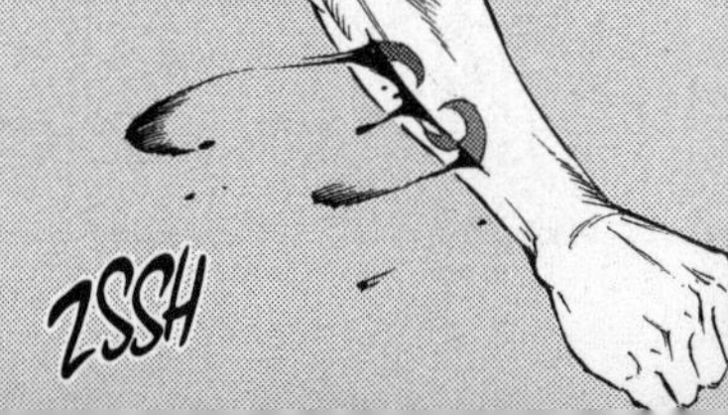
ZSSH

THAT'S MY FASTEST.
YOU NEED TO DO IT IN UNDER HALF A SECOND TO BE ABLE TO USE IT IN ACTUAL COMBAT.
ZWCH
ZSH
TRY IT.
ZWRRL
UGH!
PNNNNG
?
OW... MY CHEST STILL HURTS.
DO YOU GET THAT TOO, SENJI?

A LINGERING INJURY FROM BRANCH OF SIN?!

HMM

NEVER HEARD OF ANYTHING LIKE THAT.

HOLD ON...

SWF

HMPH!

HMMPH!

PFF

HRR

GRR

MOVE ...!

MOVE ...!

YOU'RE NOT A DEADMAN, SO GET OUTTA HERE!

AND IF YOU'RE WEARING FULL-BODY TIGHTS, STAY OUTTA MY SIGHT!

Will you get over that already?

WHOA!

HEY! GANTA!
I JUST ...

UHHH...
FOUR-EYES?!
Don't wanna see him...
THANK YOU FOR TAKING TIME OUT OF YOUR BUSY SCHEDULES TO COME HERE TODAY.
POP
HRM
WHAT'S THIS PRESS CONFERENCE ABOUT?
FLASH
HRM
WHAT'S BEHIND THE CURTAIN?
FIRST OF ALL ...
FLASH
POP
I'D LIKE TO APOLOGIZE FOR CONCEALING THE EXISTENCE OF THE UNIQUE PRISONERS KNOWN AS "DEADMEN."
FINALLY! THE TRUTH ABOUT THE UNDERGROUND BATTLE ARENA AND THE STRANGE PRISONERS.
WHUH
CONFIRMING THEIR EXISTENCE ...
HE'S GONNA RESIGN!
WHOA
MAYBE THE END OF DEADMAN WONDERLAND TOO.

THE REASON WE KEPT IT FROM THE PUBLIC IS THAT ...

...THE "DEAD-MEN"...

...ARE DANGEROUS INDIVIDUALS THAT HAVE THE INEXPLICABLE ABILITY TO CONTROL THEIR OWN BLOOD.

THEY'RE NOT ORDINARY CITIZENS.

THEIR VERY BLOOD IS DANGEROUS.

EVERY DROP COULD BE AN UNDETECTABLE WEAPON FOR MURDER AND MAYHEM.

LIVE

TO BE QUITE FRANK...

THESE INDIVIDUALS ARE NO LONGER HUMAN. THEY ARE *DANGEROUS* BEASTS.

IN THIS FACILITY WE HAVE BEEN COVERTLY SUPERVISING AND STUDYING THEM.
HOWEVER, SINCE OUR SECRETIVE WAYS HAVE CAUSED APPREHENSION, TO AVOID ANY FURTHER HINT OF IMPROPRIETY ...
...FROM NOW ON EVERYTHING WE DO WILL BE AVAILABLE TO THE PUBLIC.

WE WILL SHOW YOU THEIR TRUE NATURE AND WHY THEY CANNOT LIVE IN SOCIETY.

A PROGRAM WE CALL "CARNIVAL CORPSE"!

SHWFF
MAKE CARNIVAL CORPSE...
...OPEN TO THE PUBLIC?!
SHWF

...!!
WHO IS THAT?!

HE LOOKS LIKE...
...THE RED MAN!

CRACK
CRACK
WHO THE HELL'RE YOU? WHAT'S WITH THE MASK?

WE'RE ON NATIONAL TV, RIGHT?
ZWRG
WELL THEN...

...I AIN'T HOLDIN' NOTHIN' BACK!

SWSH

VMM

RRCH

SKWR

SHRED

A SNAKE?!
NO BRANCH OF SIN?!
CHOMP
?!

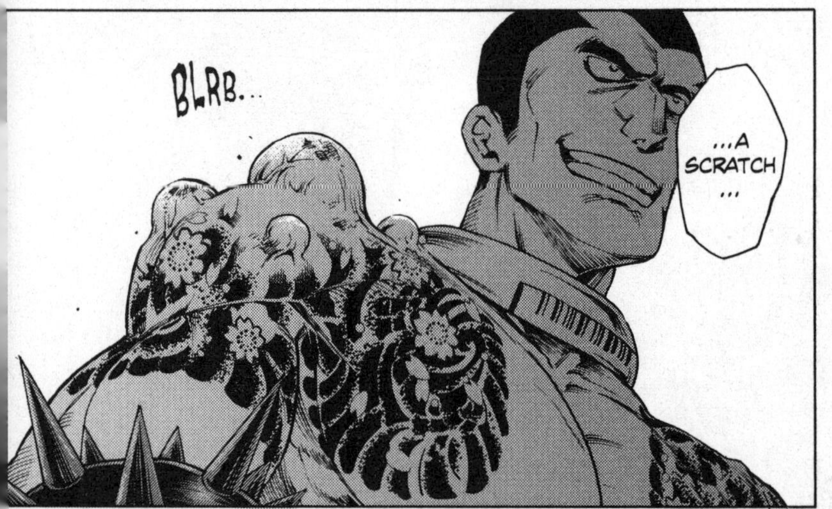

...?!
BLORG
BLRG
UH...
WH...
BORGL
WHAT ?!
HUH?!
WHAT THE HELL ?!
BLBOR
FLICK

SPLR
CH

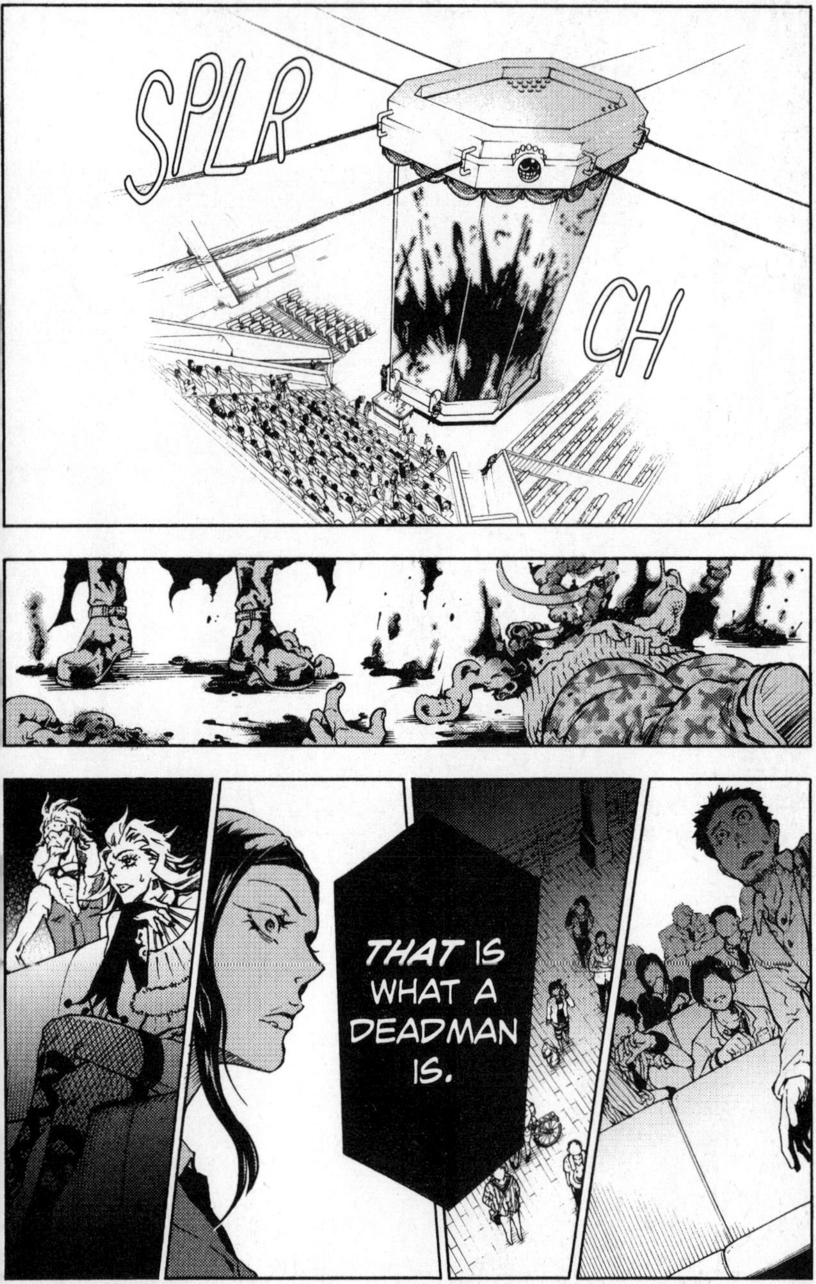

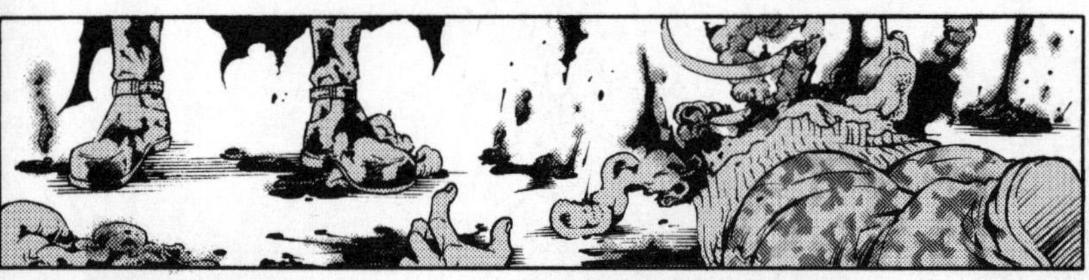

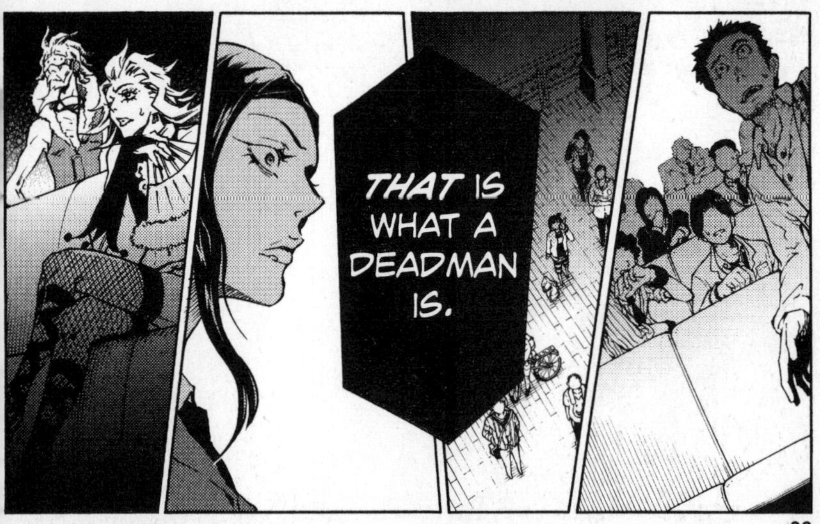
THAT IS WHAT A DEADMAN IS.

THE CONCEPT OF INNOCENCE DOES NOT APPLY TO THEM.
DO YOU UNDERSTAND NOW?
BECAUSE THEY ARE CRAZED, BLOODTHIRSTY *ANIMALS.*
URK...

THAT'S WHAT DEADMEN ARE?!
THESE GUYS'LL BE OUT ON THE STREETS IF THEY CLOSE THIS PLACE DOWN?!
WHOA
THAT'S WAY COOLER THAN WHAT'S ON THE INTERNET!
THAT WAS A PUBLIC EXECUTION! WHAT ABOUT THEIR HUMAN RIGHTS?!
MMBL
HUMAN RIGHTS ...?
YOU THINK THEY'RE HUMAN?!
SLAM
THAT FOX! STAGING A BLOOD-BATH...
...TO JUSTIFY ...
...HIS PRIVATE ARENA OF DEATH!

THERE'LL BE NO STOPPING HIM NOW!
DAMN IT!
WHO THE HELL WAS THAT GUY IN THE MASK?!
WHAT AN UNSIGHTLY, GROTESQUE BRANCH OF SIN!

...

KACH
SKACH
HYOO
HYOO!

HOP
HOP
HYOOO!!
...?

HYOO
...

TMP
NOT BAD...
YOU'RE SHAPING UP MUCH QUICKER THAN I EXPECTED.

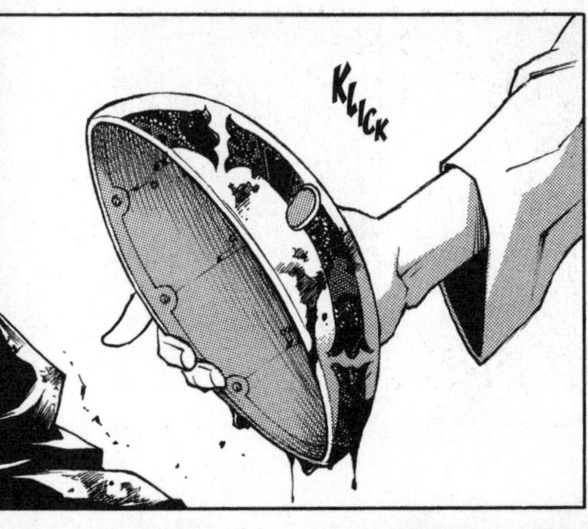
KLICK

SHK
SHVR

SHIVER
SHAKE
QUAKE

I DON'T LIKE IT.

THAT FIGHT WASN'T FOR ENTERTAINMENT OR COERCION...
HE HAD THAT GUY KILLED JUST FOR THE SAKE OF SHOWING IT.
I HAVEN'T HAD GOOSE-BUMPS LIKE THIS FOR A WHILE.

WHO WAS THAT GUY IN THE BLACK CAPE?!

NO... THERE'S NO WAY, RIGHT...?

SHF

AHA!☆
THAT WAS A "NINBEN"...
...AN ARTIFICIAL DEADMAN!

DEADMA
N WO
NDER LA
ND

KINCHO

24 Anger Song, Under Peace
M... MOCKING-BIRD?!

STAY BACK, GANTA ...
HE'S OUT OF YOUR LEAGUE!
WRCH
IT'S BEEN ...
...A LONG TIME!
SWIP

...?!
AHA!
☆
I DIDN'T COME HERE TO FIGHT.
BUT IT'S NICE TO SEE YOU STILL LOVE ME THAT MUCH.
☆
...
MOCKINGBIRD, WERE YOU ALWAYS LIKE THIS?
WH
OA
YOU USED TO BE A BIGGER FIGHT FANATIC THAN ME.

YOU WERE THE ULTIMATE DEADMAN!

LICK
...!!

...
WHAT THE-?!
TH-THAT'S S-SICK...
EWW

HUH ...?!
SHF
YOU ...
WHAT WAS THAT?!

I'VE BEEN THROUGH A LOT.
SLURP
I'M THE WEAKEST DEADMAN NOW.
CUT ME A LITTLE SLACK. ☆
CAN I LICK YOURS TOO?
SWP
CAN I...
...WOOD-PECKER?

DON'T TOUCH HIM!
W
WHOA!
AP
OH, THAT'S RIGHT, HE'S...
...IMPORTANT ISN'T HE, WRETCH— ...I MEAN, "SHIRO." ☆
I'M "MOCKINGBIRD," TOTO SAKAGAMI.
CALL ME TOTO.
NICE TO MEET YOU, "WOODPECKER."
I'M GANTA...
UM... WHAT YOU WERE SAYING EARLIER...

...ABOUT THE "NINBEN."
THAT WAS THE DEADMAN WEARING A MASK, RIGHT?
"NINBEN" MEANS "FAKE." ☆
IN OTHER WORDS, A *FAKE DEADMAN*... CREATED FOR THE PEOPLE.
THAT'S RIGHT...

...THEY HAVE NO LOVE.

WOO
WELL THEN...
IN CELEBRATION OF TOTO'S RETURN...
RAH
WELCOME BACK MOCKINGBIRD
...CHEERS!
WOO

AHA! ☆
EAT UP, EVERYONE! LET'S CELEBRATE!
ACCEPT MY LOVE! ☆
WAS MOCKINGBIRD ALWAYS LIKE THIS?
HOO
YAH
WHO CARES? IT'S FREE BOOZE!
FORGET CARNIVAL CORPSE.
JUST ENJOY BEING OUTSIDE.

YOU GUYS WANNA SEE SOME-THIN'?!
AH
AW, CRAP! CROW'S WASTED!
TRAPE-ZIUS MUSCLE PUMP!
FLEX

ARTIFICIAL DEADMEN?

BUT THAT WAS ...

IT CAN'T BE!
I HOPE IT WAS JUST A COINCIDENCE... OR MY MISTAKE...
PLUS...
THE WAY SHE LOOKED...

WHAT'S WRONG? NOT HAVING FUN?
OH... TOTO!
STILL THINKING ABOUT THE NINBEN?

...
WHEN I SAW THE NINBEN... IT KINDA REMINDED ME OF...
...THE *RED MAN* ...

CLAP
RED...? OH...
THE WRETCHED EGG, HUH?
THEY *DO* LOOK SIMILAR. ☆

WHAT?

Y-YOU'VE SEEN HIM?!
HMM? YEAH.

THAT'S RIGHT...
HMPH
YOU DON'T KNOW ANYTHING ABOUT THAT AWFUL...
...?
YOU'VE GOT IT ALL WRONG, GANTA.
THAT LITTLE NINBEN AND THE WRETCHED EGG ARE ONLY SIMILAR ON THE SURFACE.

THE WRETCHED EGG IS ONE OF A KIND.
IT'S THE BEGINNING AND END TO ALL SINS.
COMEDY AND TRAGEDY, STRENGTH AND WEAKNESS, LIFE AND DEATH, LOVE AND HATE... THE LOVE THAT CONTAINS *ALL* CONTRADICTIONS!
HE... HE KNOWS THE RED MAN?!
THINK BACK, WOOD-PECKER.
THE WRETCHED EGG IS...
HOUG

SHIRO!
HEH HEH HEH.
FOUND YOU, GANTA!
HEY!
QUIT RUBBING UP AGAINST ME.
Are you drunk?
THERE'S ONLY SO MUCH A GUY CAN TAKE!
AH, YOUNG LOVE!
I'M SO JEALOUS!
Just pretend I'm a tree.
NO, IT'S NOT LIKE THAT!
WE'RE JUST FRIENDS!

☆

WAIT, THERE'S MORE I WANT TO ASK YOU...

...

WHAT? WHAT?

...

YOU'RE SO LUCKY. YOU ALWAYS SEEM TO BE HAVING FUN.

HMM?

CUZ NOW I HAVE YOU! NOT LIKE BEFORE!

THAT'S ALL I NEED TO HAVE FUN!

AM I HAVING FUN...?

NOT LIKE BEFORE...

YEAH ...
... I AM.
OH!
BUT IT'S NO FUN IF THERE'S NO SNACKS!
SO IT'S SNACKS OVER ME, EH?
I should've known.
I CAME UP WITH A NEW RECIPE...
HONEY RAMEN!
I'LL PASS!
CHIRP
CHIRP

BREE
BREE
BREE
UNGH...
SMACK
IS IT MORNING ALREADY ...?
BREE
BREE
BREE
SIGH...
I AM *SO* HUNG OVER...

...!

WHEN DID THEY ...?

FROM THE NINBEN?

AN INVITATION TO CARNIVAL CORPSE?

AT G-R 93... TIME...

HMM ...?

PLIP

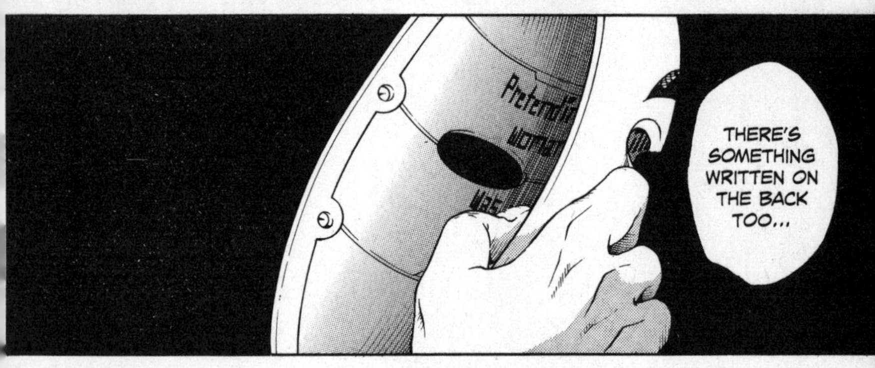

SO? WHEN DO I GET TO DISSECT THIS WRETCHED EGG?
THE FILES SAY THAT WRETCHED EGG LIVES AMONG THE PRISONERS. AND SHE'S A GIRL, TOO!
I WONDER WHAT SHE LOOKS LIKE?
BLUSH
AH!
WHAT SHE LOOKS LIKE WHEN SHE'S CRYING?

AS LONG AS WE CAN STOP "MOTHER GOOSE," WE CAN DRAW HER OUT ANYTIME WE WANT.
BUT THERE'S NO GUARANTEE THAT WHAT HAPPENED TEN YEARS AGO WON'T HAPPEN AGAIN.

IT'S STILL A BIT TOO SOON.
OH... HOW SAD.

BY THE WAY...

WHAT DO THE MESSAGES ON THE BACKS OF THE MASKS MEAN?

OH...

IT'S JUST A LITTLE CHALLENGE.

JUST SPICING IT UP WITH A BIT OF ***DESPAIR, FEAR*** AND ***ANGER*** FOR THOSE BATTLE-HARDENED VETERANS.

I NEED THEM TO FIGHT WITH EVERYTHING THEY HAVE.

I DON'T CARE IF IT'S THE NINBEN OR THEM...

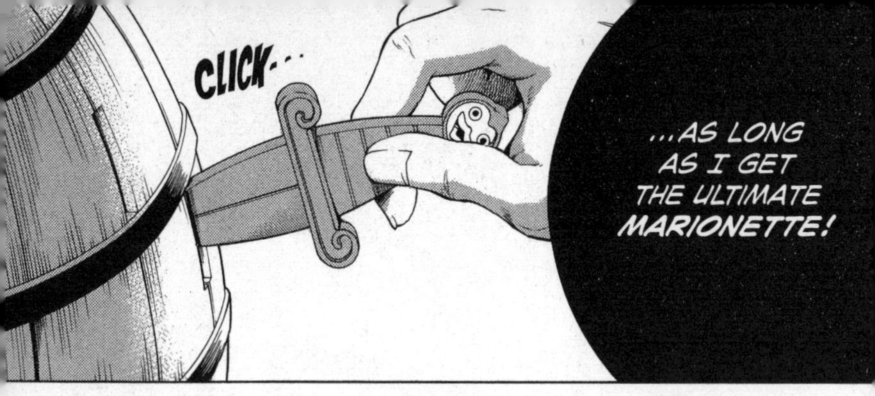
...AS LONG AS I GET THE ULTIMATE MARIONETTE!
CLICK...

KTAK
...
HOW DID THEY...?
DSNAK
CHAK
SUKE-GAWA...
IT SEEMS SOMETHING'S WRITTEN HERE. CAN YOU READ IT FOR ME?
I DON'T THINK YOU WANT TO KNOW.
WHAT THE HELL...
...IS THIS?

Mommy ran away
Threw away the flowers and ran away
Left her daughter and ran away ♪
Crow Claw is a Branch of Sin ♪
A Branch of Sin that killed four friends ♪
Pretending to be a slut
The woman you killed was very beautiful
Pretending, pretending to hide her ugliness ♪

Your broken daughter screams energetically
Cover your ears, but you can still hear
Cover your eyes, but she's still broken ♪
Lots of friends ♪
Loved by a Red Man
Thanks to that, lots of severed heads ♪

SCREW THIS!

TROMP

TROMP

WARD G R93...

TROMP

TROMP

IN YOUR ROOM TOO?

WHAT DID IT SAY?

I DON'T EVEN WANNA REPEAT IT!

THAT MASKED SCUMBAG!

G-R93

WHRRR
G-R
I LIKE THE LOOK OF THIS.
KA CHAK
CREEEAK
G-R

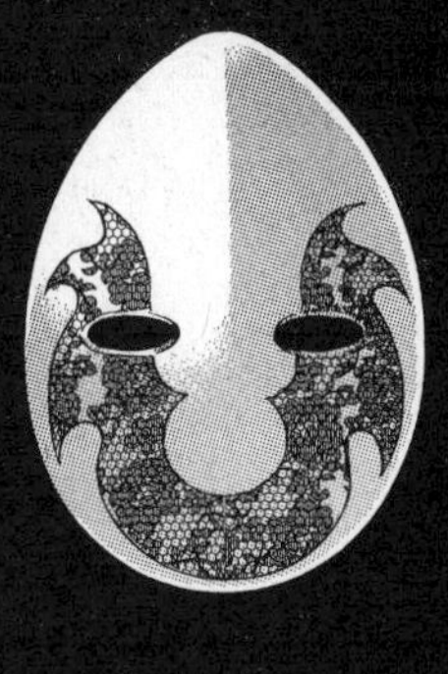
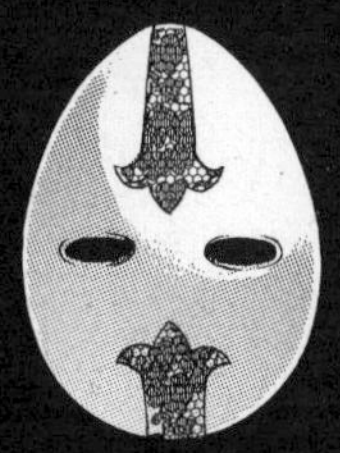

...?
WHAT THE--?
IT'S PITCH DARK...
WOOO

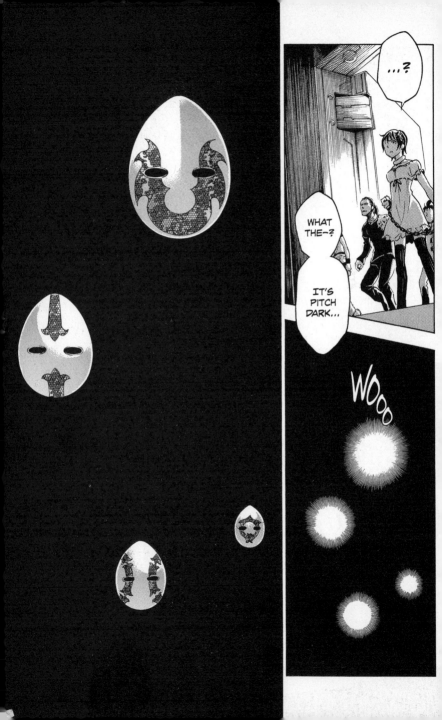

PCHH
!!!
AAA
THMP
THMP
THMP

SLITHER...

WH UH?

...

BZZZ

LADIES AND GENTLEMEN AND ANYONE ELSE STILL UP AT THIS FRIGHTFUL HOUR...

WHRRRRR

PRESENTED BY:
GOUT HANDCUFFS
...YOU PROBABLY WON'T BE SLEEPING A WINK TONIGHT! WILL THIS BE A HAPPY DREAM FOR YOU OR A NIGHTMARE? WELCOME TO THE LAND OF THE DEAD...
A
A
A
A
OUR VERY FIRST ROUND IS A TEAM COMPETITION.
PLEASE LOOK AT YOUR SCREEN...

WAA
WELCOME TO CARNIVAL CORPSE!
...READ THEIR PROFILES... ENJOY THEIR MADNESS!
GRRR...
SWCH
THAT *BASTARD!*
18

FIGHT!!

KILL.

TWITCH

SHING

WITH PLEASURE.

ZWORP
!!!
WATCH OUT FOR THOSE SNAKES!

SSS...
... SLICE!
WHOA
WAY TO GO, SENJI!
HEY!
LEAVE SOME FOR ME, CROW!

?!
WHAT'S THAT GUY DOING?
HOW CAN HE MOVE AFTER TAKING THAT KIND OF DAMAGE?!
SENJI ...!

...!!

DAMN!

BLRB

SLICE

ARRRGH!

THAT HURT!

WHY THE HELL ARE YOU ATTACKING ME?!

GET ON YOUR KNEES AND THANK ME, MUSCLE-HEAD.
HUH?!
YOU'RE SO DAMNED DUMB.
THOSE BRANCH OF SIN SNAKES ARE *VENOMOUS*.
IF IT SPREADS, ALL YOUR VAUNTED MUSCLES WILL BUBBLE UP *LIKE THAT*.
...!
BLRG
URGH ...
H-HELP ...
BLRBL

SWIP
HELP ...
HRMM
KILL ...
FEELS GOOD.
HRMM
FEELS GOOD... FEELS GOOD.
KILL, KILL, KILL.

KILL, KILL, KILL, KILL, KILL, FEELS GOOD, KILL, KILL, KILL, KILL, KILL, FEELS GOOD KILL, KIL
KILL, KILL, KILL, KILL, KILL, KILL, KILL, KILL, KILL, KILL, KILL, KIL
KILL, KILL, KILL, KILL, FEELS GOOD, KILL, KILL, KILL, KILL, KILL, KILL, KILL, KIL
FEELS GOOD, KILL, KILL, KILL, KILL, KILL, KILL, KILL, KILL KILL, KILL KILL, KIL
SSS..
SLITHER
WH...
WH...
WHAAAA!!

DWAK
KLANG

MASK ...
MASK ...

MASK ...

CLICK.

FEELS GOOOOD ...

KILL, KILL, KILL, KILL, KILL.
KILL, KILL, KILL.
ZWORP
ZWORP
ZWORP
KILL.

GANTA! DON'T JUST STAND THERE!

AZAMI...

LAND LAND

ADMAN DEADMAN DEAD

R WONDER WONDER

LAND LAND

ADMAN DEADMAN DEAD
R WONDER WONDER
LAND LAND
ADMAN DEADMAN DEAD
R WONDER WONDER
LAND LAND
ADMAN DEADMAN DEAD
R WONDER WONDER
LAND LAND
ADMAN DEADMAN DEAD
R WONDER WONDER
LAND LAND
ADMAN DEADMAN DEAD
R WONDER WONDER
LAND LAND
ADMAN DEADMAN DEAD
R WONDER WONDER
LAND LAND
ADMAN DEADMAN DEAD
R WONDER WONDER
LAND LAND
ADMAN DEADMAN DEAD
R WONDER WONDER
LAND LAND

XL

25 Failure Firing
YOU'RE KIDDING ME, RIGHT ...?
AZAMI ...
SWIP

25 Failure Firing

Z
?!
WH-WHAT JUST HAPPENED?
DID YOU SEE THAT?!
N-NO...
WHO IS THAT? HE'S NOT ON THE FIGHT CARD!
...!
I DON'T REMEMBER INVITING HIM.

INTER-
ESTING...
SO HE'S STILL ALIVE.
THE WINNER OF CARNIVAL CORPSE FROM TWO YEARS AGO...
THE ONLY DEADMAN TO EVER FACE WRETCHED EGG...
SEARCH
no.5580
MOCKINGBIRD...
...TOTO SAKIGAMI...
TOTO...
HOW KIND OF THE *ULTIMATE* TO LEND US A HAND...
SL
ICH
HOPE YOU STILL GOT YOUR SKILLS, MOCKINGBIRD!

DON'T WORRY ABOUT ME, BOYS.
AS LONG AS THIS BODY LASTS...
...I'LL BLOW THEM AWAY WITH THE POWER OF MY LOVE. ☆
!!
DAMN IT, NOT NOW... MY CHEST ...
URGH... TOTO... WATCH OUT...
LOVE ☆ LABY-RINTH ...
ZWRR

CROW CLAW!!

...

?!
TH-THAT LOOKS LIKE...!
GRRR...
COPYING MY MOVES WITHOUT PERMISSION!

MOCKINGBIRDS ARE EXPERTS AT MIMICKING OTHERS. ☆
BUT I'VE HAD MY RESET BUTTON PRESSED, SO...
...I CAN ONLY USE THE CROW CLAW THAT I SAW YESTERDAY...
!
ZWRR
ONK

KRCH
SPLAT
CAW
Whaddaya mean, "only"?!
WOW!
THAT WAS QUICK!
OOOHHH!
HAS MOCKINGBIRD'S UNEXPECTED ARRIVAL TURNED THE TIDE?!

KRAK
WHIP
KRAK
WHIP
UH... HE'S ALREADY DEAD.
YEAH?
WHO CARES?!
MAKING FUN OF OTHERS' TRAUMA!
JUST DYING ONCE ISN'T ENOUGH!!

DAMNED RIGHT!
SQU
NOW THEY'RE DEAD AND UGLY!
ASH
HELL YEAH.
THAT'S WHAT MY DAUGHTER SAYS.
SNAP
FWSH
DOOSH
FWH

TWO TO GO!
THEN IT'S TIME FOR US...
RRIP
...!
...TO END ALL THIS TALK OF LOVE. ☆
!

NO...!!
GUYS, WAIT...
DING
...THAT'S...

...AZAMI...!
SKRRK
?!
SKNNN

DO

DW
EEEE

WHAT THE-?
WHAT JUST HAPPENED?!
DID IT BREAK?! IT'S NOT SHOWING ANYTHING!
BAM
HUH
HEY! PUT IT BACK ON!
WHUH

DIREC-TOR TAMAKI!
WE'RE GETTING COMPLAINTS ABOUT THE FEED DROPPING OUT...
THE MAIN CAMERA AND THE PERIPHERAL SYSTEMS ARE ALL DOWN.
DIREC-TOR TAMAKI?!
WAS THAT... BRANCH OF SIN?!

DID THAT BOY...?
THE BROADCAST IS CANCELED.

BUT HOW...? DID HIS BRANCH OF SIN EVOLVE?
THE NAMELESS WORM THAT WRETCHED EGG PERSONALLY IMPLANTED... THE **RED DIAMOND**... COULD THAT BE THE CAUSE?!

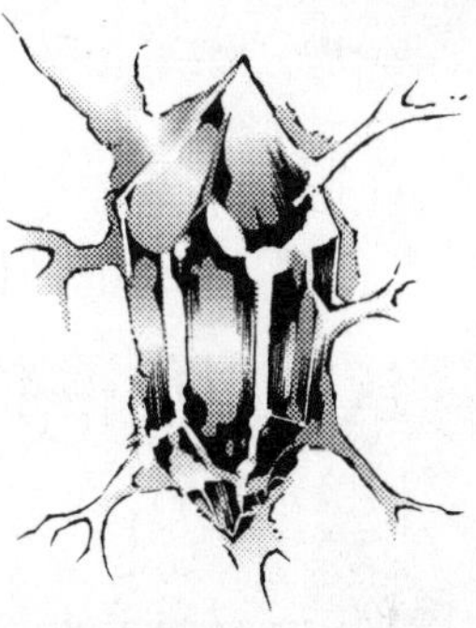

C-CANCELED?!

FORGET ABOUT THAT...

I NEED ANOTHER LOOK THROUGH GANTA IGARASHI'S DATA!

WOODPECKER

ON LINE
BEEP
HEY!
WHAT THE HELL IS GOING ON?
THE CARNIVAL CORPSE PROGRAM IS AN UTTER FAILURE!
ON LINE
NO...
THE EXPERIMENT WAS A HUGE SUCCESS!
WE'VE STUMBLED ON TO SOMETHING HERE...
PWNG!
UGHH...

WH-WHAT HAPPENED?
WHERE'S AZAMI...?
KTAK
SHE'S ALIVE!
GOOD!
GANTA, WHAT...
...WHAT WERE YOU THINKING?!

HUH ...?

WAIT ...
I DID THIS?

DEADMAN WONDER

LAND

DEADMAN WONDER

LAND

DEADMAN WONDER

LAND

G
26 Blue Sky with Blue Devils
KEEP OUT
KEEP OUT
KEEP

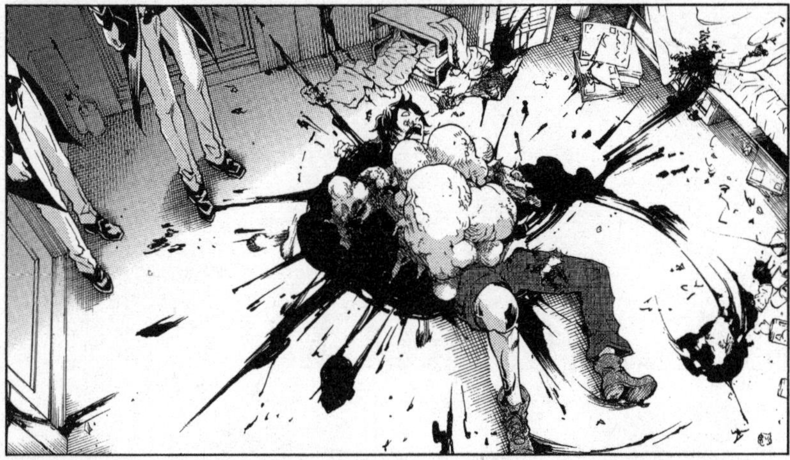

TUG

WHAT DO YOU THINK?
I BELIEVE THEY MEET YOUR REQUIREMENT FOR AN "OBEDIENT SPECIAL ABILITIES UNIT."
FINE. I'LL AMEND THE BUDGET.
THE NINBEN MAY CERTAINLY BE USEFUL AS A PENAL SQUAD.
ON LINE
DEAD

BUT NO MORE BLUNDERS LIKE CARNIVAL CORPSE THREE DAYS AGO.
BEEP
OFF LINE
...
RIGHT.
A PENAL SQUAD?
WHAT AN AWFULLY ANACHRONISTIC IDEA.
TURNING CRIMINALS INTO DISPOSABLE SOLDIERS.
TYPICAL MILITARY INEFFICIENCY. BUT...
WHO CARES AS LONG AS WE GET RESEARCH FUNDING.
"BLUNDER" MY FOOT!

"HUMPTY DUMPTY"...

WILL IT BE THE WOODPECKER THAT CRACKS THE EGG?

GASP

TH- THREE DAYS ...?

SKF

I BETTER EAT MY CANDY!

...

WHY WAS I SLEEPING ...?

CHOMP

UM...

...!

WHERE'S AZAMI?!

AZAMI?

SHUF

SHE'S MY FRIEND...

A FRIEND?
I'M YOUR FRIEND, GANTA.
YEAH!
BUT THIS IS IMPORTANT TOO!
UMM... IF I CAN FIND WHERE THE NINBEN ARE...
SHIRO, CAN YOU HELP ME FIND AZAMI?
YOU KNOW THIS PLACE INSIDE AND OUT!
SURE...
ANYTHING FOR YOU, GANTA!
...

AND I'VE RECENTLY LEARNED HOW TO DO THAT THING!
CHNNN
?
THAT THING?

SO *THIS* IS WHERE YOU WERE HIDING HIM, SHIRO!

CLAP

TOTO...
... WHADDYA MEAN "HIDE"?

OH, NOTHING... BUT YOU REALLY SHOULD STAY IN HERE.
GANTA...

DON'T YOU REMEMBER WHAT YOU DID THREE DAYS AGO?

...!

DIDN'T YOU HEAR?

KEEP OU
ANOTHER DEADMAN WAS KILLED.
WHO DO THOSE NINBEN THINK THEY ARE?!
KEE
OUT
MOST OF OUR TOUGHEST GUYS WERE INJURED IN THE CARNIVAL CORPSE.
IT WAS THAT KID, RIGHT?

YEAH, THAT TRAITOR!

HF...

HUF

THAT'S RIGHT...

...I ENDED UP HURTING ***EVERYONE!***

I'M SORRY!
...
HMMM?
SO YOUR BRANCH OF SIN MANIFESTED UNINTENTIONALLY?
YOU'RE TOUGH WITH YOUR GANTA GUN...
...NO...
...YOUR "GANBARU GUN"...
"GANBARU"...?
HUH?!
HUH?
...You changed the name again?!
WELL, UH...
I STILL CAN'T CONTROL MY GANBARU GUN.
THAT DAY...

...A FRIEND OF MINE WAS ONE OF THE NINBEN.
SO I WAS DESPERATE ...
YOU CALL THOSE TURDS...
...FRIENDS ?!
WHAT?
OH, NO!
SHE'S NOT USUALLY THAT KIND OF PERSON.
SOMETHING WAS WRONG.
THERE'S GOTTA BE A REASON ...
HEH ...
FLEX
HEH HEH ...
I LIKE THAT...

I... NO...
IT PROBABLY WASN'T JUST ME...
AFTER I SAW WHAT WAS WRITTEN INSIDE THAT MASK...
...I WAS DESPERATE TO SLICE THOSE GUYS INTO A THOUSAND PIECES!

I'VE GOTTEN SO SOFT 'CAUSE OF YOU.
PLIP
BEFORE, I WOULD'VE STABBED YOU WITHOUT HESITATION.
GET OUTTA HERE, WOODPECKER ...
...OR I JUST MIGHT KILL *YOU* INSTEAD OF YOUR FRIEND.

SPLOOSH

SORRY, BUT...

...I'M IN NO MOOD TO LISTEN TO SOME KID WHO STILL SMELLS LIKE HIS MOTHER'S TITS.

SLAM

LET ME PUT IT THIS WAY...

IF YOU HADN'T STOPPED US FROM KILLING THE NINBEN, MY DRINKING BUDDY WOULD STILL BE ALIVE.

SLUFFF
WELL, YOU'RE LOOKING GOOD...
OH, THIS?
IT'S NOTHING...
I JUST... UH... FELL.

NO ONE CARES HOW YOU GOT HURT.
FWFF
YO...
...
THAT WOUND ...
DID I...?
DON'T WORRY ABOUT IT...
IT'S LIKE THAT WOUND ON MY BACK I SHOWED YOU ONCE.
WHEN YOU FIGHT DOWN HERE, YOU END UP WITH SCARS.

BECAUSE ...
...YOU CAN'T TRUST ANY-ONE!
THANKS FOR REMINDING ME.
...
WAIT, MINA-
WUMP

G
SLAM

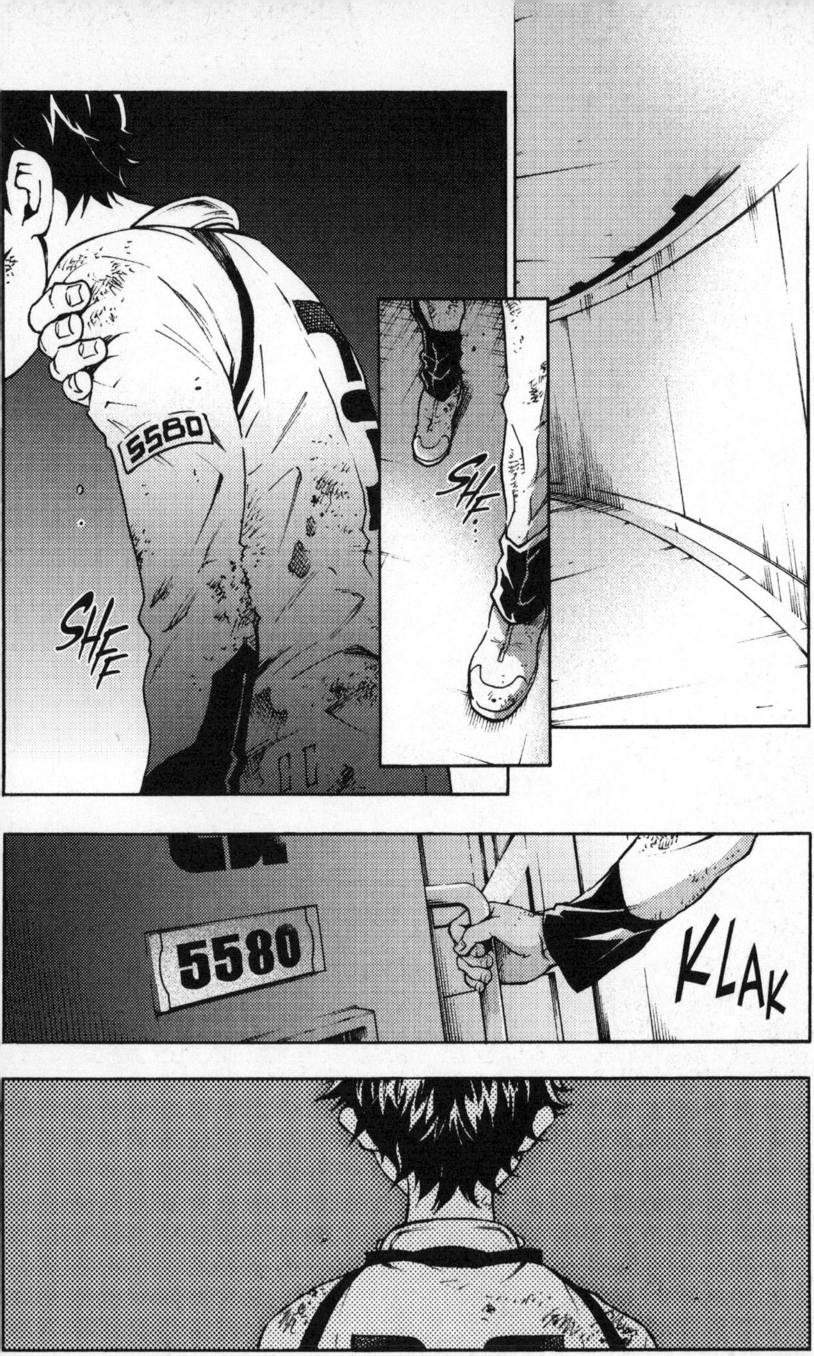

SHFF

5580

SHFF

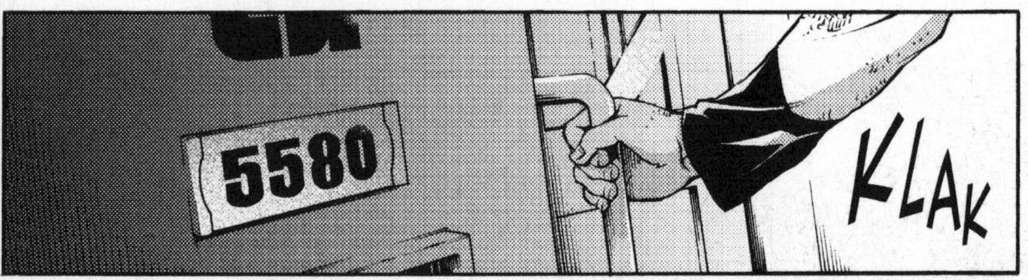

DIE
TRAITOR
FUCK MOTHER OF FUCK

AHA!☆

YOU SHOULDN'T HAVE COME BACK HERE.

SHIRO WAS TRYING KEEP YOU FROM SEEING THIS.

...

IS THIS ...?

YOU HEARD, DIDN'T YOU?

RIGHT NOW, THE DEADMEN ARE IN A RACE FOR SURVIVAL WITH THOSE LOVELESS NINBEN... WE'RE "EXPERIMENTAL SUBJECTS"...

TEMPERS ARE RUNNING HIGH.

LITTLE BIRDS SHIVERING WITH FEAR AND ANGER.

BECAUSE JUST BEING A DEADMAN MEANS THERE'S A CHANCE THEY'RE GOING TO COME FOR YOU NEXT.

HEY, GANTA...
TELL ME...
WHOSE SIDE DO YOU WANT TO BE ON?

...
I WANT TO BE ON THE SIDE OF JUSTICE.
AHA!☆

THAT'S AN AWFULLY FLIMSY DREAM. ☆

HEY, TAKE A LOOK AT THAT.
WHOA ...

AREN'T YOU THAT DEADMAN KID FROM UNDER-GROUND?
THE ONE THAT LOST IT ON THE BROADCAST.

YEAH. SO WHAT ...?

SONOF-ABITCH DEAD-MAN!
POW
GOD-DAMN PLAGUE!
WE AIN'T AFRAID OF YOU!
BOOF
BECAUSE OF YOU MONSTERS, PEOPLE THINK WE'RE DANGEROUS, TOO!
YOU SCUM!
CRACK
WUMP
WHAM

HEY...

THE WEATHER SURE IS NICE...

HAIII-YA!
ACEMAN HAS ARRIVED!
GYAAA!
STOP PICKING ON GANTA!
POWERFUL ILLUSION POLYPHENOL ENDLESS SPOILED BRAT PUNCH!
WHOA! WHO THE HELL IS SHE?!
WHAM
BAM
SLAM
HEEEELP
AIYOW
OWCH
Ai!
AAGH!
WE WON'T FORGET THIS, BITCH!
RARR

GANTA! YOU OKAY?
ON THE SIDE OF JUSTICE ...?
YUP.
I'M ON ***YOUR*** SIDE!

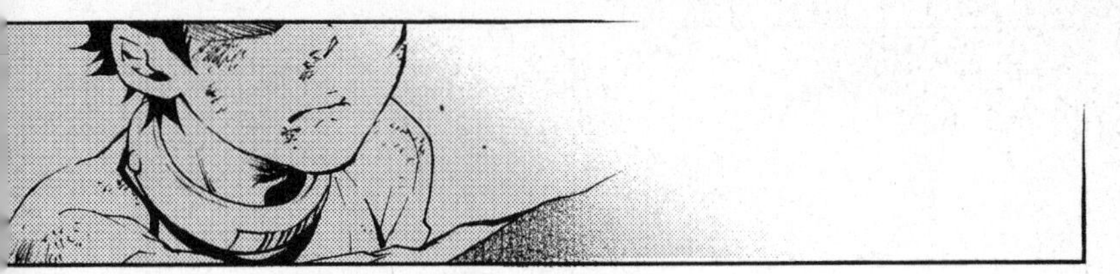

THANKS
...

SNFF
...
C'MON, GET UP! LET'S GO HELP YOUR FRIEND!
HEY, LOOK HERE!
HERE! HERE!
...?
ZWRR
ZWSH

B-B-BRANCH OF SIN ...?!

Y-YOU ...
... YOU'RE A DEAD-MAN TOO?!
IS THAT WHY YOU'RE IN HERE?!
SEE?
I'LL BE MORE USEFUL FROM NOW ON!

LET'S GO, GANTA!
SHIRO'S ...
...A DEAD-MAN?
GANTA ...?

...
GO AWAY!
I DON'T WANT ANY HELP FROM A DEADMAN.

?
GANTA! WAIT!
SMACK

I'M NOT GOING WITH YOU, AND...
...YOU AREN'T COMING WITH ME.
I'M GOING ALONE!

WHAT...? GANTA, WAIT!
WHY ARE YOU...
I DON'T UNDER-STAND!
...
LET ME PUT IT THIS WAY...

I'M TELLING YOU THAT I *HATE* YOU NOW.

SKF
...
WMP
PLIP
PLIP
W-W-W-W...

WAAAA

WAAAAAAA

DEADMAN WONDERLAND 6

Jinsei Kataoka
Kazuma Kondou

STAFF

Karaiko
Ryuichi Saitaniya
Shinji Sato
Taro Tsuchiya
Taku Nakamura
Toshihiro Noguchi

CONTINUED IN VOLUME 7

DEADMAN WONDERLAND VOLUME 6!
THE CREDITS!
Cookies?
FIRST OF ALL ...
ART AND CHARACTERS...
JINSEI KATAOKA.
SETTING AND DESIGN, KAZUMA KONDOU.
NEXT UP...

...THE STAFF.

RYUICHI SAITANI-YA.

SHINJI SATO.

TARO TSUCHIYA, TAKU NAKA-MURA!

TOSHIHIRO NOGUCHI.

THASS ALL FER THE STAFF LIST!

YOU'RE NOT SAYING IT RIGHT!

DEADMAN WONDERLAND

DEADMAN WONDERLAND
VOLUME 6
VIZ MEDIA EDITION

STORY & ART BY
JINSEI KATAOKA, KAZUMA KONDOU

TRANSLATION/JOE YAMAZAKI
ENGLISH ADAPTATION/STAN!
TOUCH-UP ART & LETTERING/JAMES GAUBATZ
DESIGN/SAM ELZWAY
EDITOR/MIKE MONTESA, JENNIFER LEBLANC

PRINTED IN THE U.S.A.

PUBLISHED BY VIZ MEDIA, LLC
P.O. BOX 77010
SAN FRANCISCO, CA 94107

10 9 8 7 6 5 4 3 2 1
FIRST PRINTING, DECEMBER 2014

www.viz.com

PARENTAL ADVISORY
DEADMAN WONDERLAND is rated T+ and is recommended for older teens. This volume contains scenes of supernatural horror and violence, and suggestive themes.

ratings.viz.com

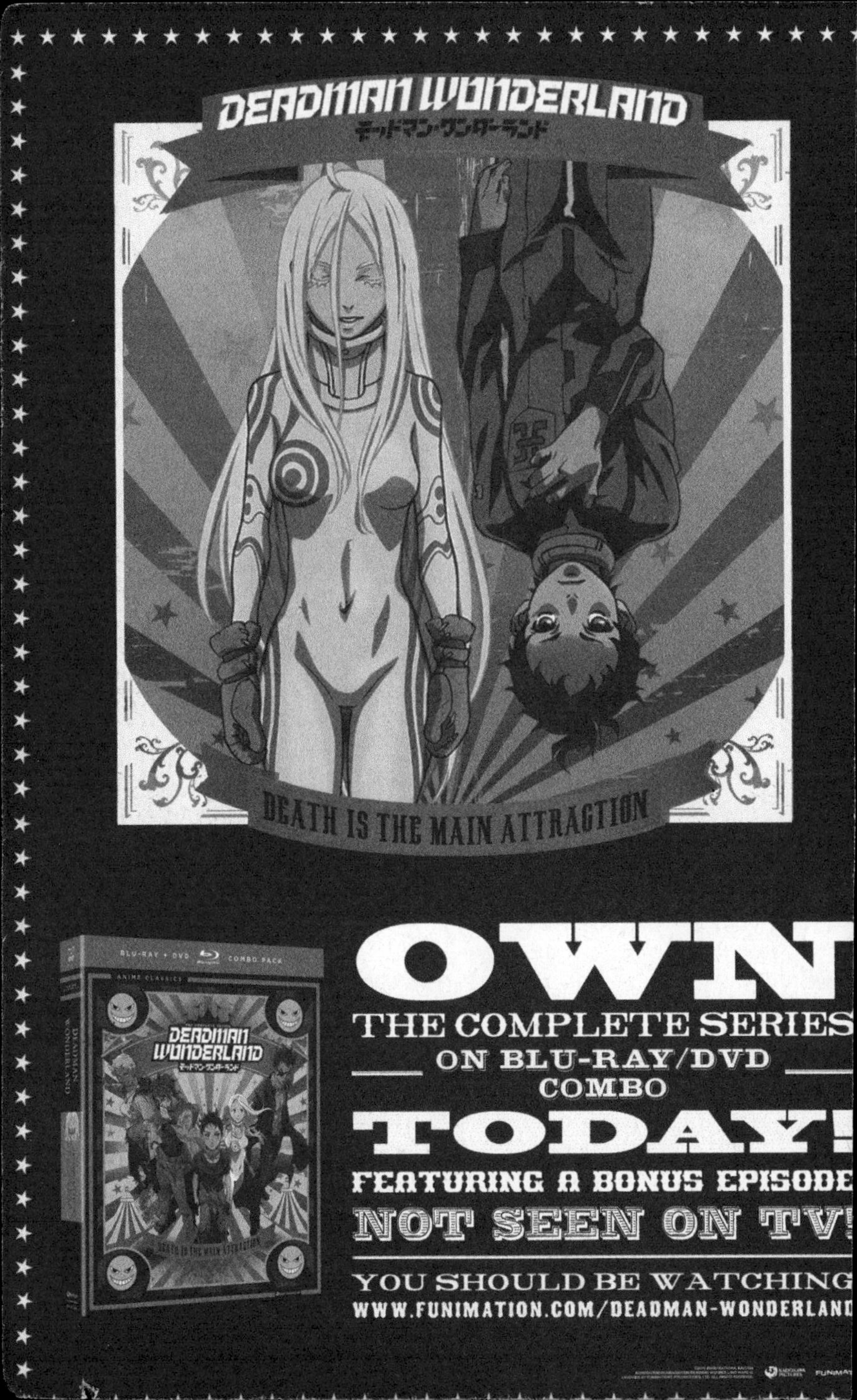

Hey! You're Reading in the Wrong Direction!

This is the ***end*** of this graphic novel!

To properly enjoy this VIZ graphic novel, please turn it around and begin reading from ***right to left.*** Unlike English, Japanese is read right to left, so Japanese comics are read in reverse order from the way English comics are typically read.

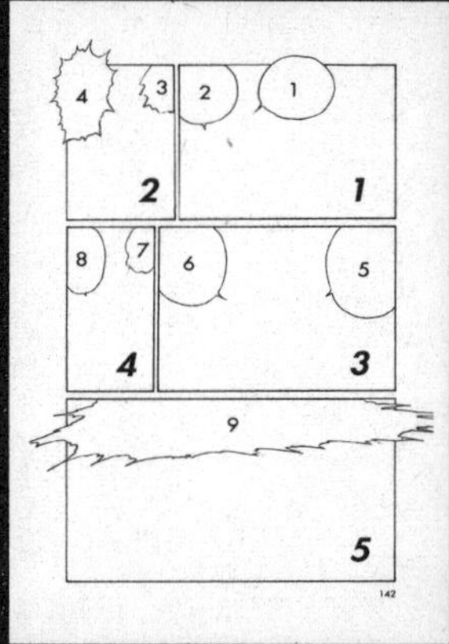

Follow the action this way

This book has been printed in the original Japanese format in order to preserve the orientation of the original artwork. Have fun with it!